GLOUCESTERSHIRE DIALECT

A selection of words and anecdotes
from around Gloucestershire

by
Eve Chipping

BRADWELL
BOOKS

1

Published by Bradwell Books
9 Orgreave Close Sheffield S13 9NP
Email: books@bradwellbooks.co.uk

British Library Cataloguing in Publication Data:
a catalogue record for this book is available from the British Library.

1st Edition

ISBN: 9781910551158

Design by: Andrew Caffrey

Print: Gomer Press, Llandysul, Ceredigion SA44 4JL

Image Credits: iStock, Creative Commons & pastandpresentpublications.com

Introduction

From cheese to wool to KING ALFRED THE GREAT, Gloucestershire has long been recognised for its contribution to the world. But there's even more to the county, not least its fascinating dialect! Whether it is the speech of the New Forest, the language of Gloucester or its many quirky local idioms, you'll find a *'bundation'* of things to discover in this book! Relax and you'll see that it's no *'limb'* to explore the local dialect! You can also get to know some fascinating local sayings from the past.

The village of Broadway, situated in the far southeast of Worcestershire, very close to the Gloucestershire border. iStock

Gloucestershire is a place of contrasts that are just as interesting as its dialect. It's little wonder that so many writers and poets (dialect and otherwise) have been inspired by this place, from LAURIE LEE to DENNIS POTTER to F.W. HARVEY. You can also find out why Gloucestershire's most famous folk song is widely believed to hide a secret political message. If you want history, you'll discover it in the county's links with ALFRED THE GREAT, the Domesday Book, the world's first lawnmower and much more! If you're looking for literature, you'll find it in words and songs that have enchanted and intrigued people all over the world. You'll also uncover some surprising links with the world's best-loved doctor and boy wizard!

You can also learn why lions used to roam the hillsides of the Cotswolds and why the Gloucestershire dialect is spoken in the South Pacific. Plus, you can read about how two of our best-loved Christmas songs – and the American national anthem – have their roots in this county... **So if you'd like to know more about Gloucestershire and the language of its people, read on!**

About Gloucestershire

Gloucestershire stretches all the way from just north of Bristol and the Severn Vale to the Cotswold Hills, covering the Forest of Dean, Cheltenham and Gloucester. It is divided into three parts: the majority of the Cotswolds, the Severn Vale and the Royal Forest of Dean, and the Severn Vale and has a population of around 565,000 people.

Pronouncing Gloucestershire dialect

The letter *'A'* is pronounced *'AH'* in repeating the alphabet. In Gloucester and some other parts of the county the long *A* is pronounced *'EE'* by the middle classes; thus, *'I'll take a halfpenny cake for the baby'* becomes *'I'll teek an eepennykeek for the beeby'*. On the other hand, the broad *A* sound as in *'father'* is frequently further broadened into *'AW'*; thus, *'the spaw'*, *'a fawthing'*.

In some parts of the Hundred of Berkeley the *A* does not have the long broad sound of *'father'*, but the short *A* of the German *'mann'*. In this way all words ending in *'ange'* are pronounced as *'change'*, *'range'*, *'mange'*, *'strange'*, *'danger'* etc.; that is, like *'flange'*, but with the above short broad *A*.

Glossary

All creatures great and small

Aichee or akee – hedge sparrow

Artishrew or artistrow – harvest mouse.

Asgall – newt

Asker – newt

Ayfer – heifer

Banner – stickleback

Banty – stickleback or minnow

Barrow-pig – hog

Bittle – beetle

Black steer or stare – starling

Blue hawk – sparrow hawk

Blue Isaac – hedge sparrow

Body – the place next to the foremost horse in a team

Body-horse – the second horse of a team

Botcher – a salmon trout

Bout – a rabbit's burrow

Brawn – a boar pig

Brown hawk – kestrel

Breeze, briz – gadfly

Brim – boar pig

Buzzock – a donkey

Cam ewes – sea gulls

Catterpillar – cockchafer
Church pigs – woodlice
Colley – the blackbird
Fitchet – ferret
Flitter-mouse – bat
Galligantus – any animal larger than the average
Hartistraw – the harvest mouse
Knacker – a collier's horse
Laughing betsy – the green woodpecker
Leathern bat – the common bat
Maggot – magpie
May-fish – a fish which was found in the Severn River at certain times of the year. It was also known as also the 'twait'.
Oodle – the nightingale
Oontitump – a molehill
Phaizan – a pheasant
Pitcher – a pole cat

Food and drink

Adry – thirsty
Bib – a small drink, a sup
Bibble – to drink, tipple
Bottle – a small wooden cask-shaped vessel which held a person's beer
Brashy or braishy – applied to beer which tastes both

mild and hard. Also used to describe mealy potatoes!

Bannut – walnut

Bathe – to toast

Bezzle – to squander money on drink

Cheese cowl – a tub in which cheese is made

Cheese ladder – the support for the milk sieve over the cooler

Cherry curds – the same as 'beestings': the first milk after calving

Dough kiver – the trough in which dough is made

Draught – 'mind your draught' means take another glass

Drink – beer or cider

Dump – a dumpling

Dunch dumpling – a hard or plain pudding, made of flour and water

Elevens – eleven o'clock lunch for workmen

Fammel – to be famished

Feggy dump – plum pudding

Fittle – victuals

Fresh – half-intoxicated

Fret – a gaseous fermentation of cider or beer

Frog – a tipsy person is said to be like a frog in a fit

Hedgepigs – the berries of the sloe

Heel – the top crust of a loaf or the rind on the sides of a cheese

Honger – hunger

Hongered – hungry

Hop-about – apple dumpling

Huff – light pastry or pie crust

Huff cap – a pear used to make perry

Jerry house or shop – a beer house

Junk – a tasty dish, a hash or stew

Leer – empty, hungry

Levence – dough set for fermentation

Liquorish – sweet, luscious

Mesheroom or mesheroon – mushroom

Moochers – blackberries

Moochering – blackberrying: 'Moocher, moocher, blackberry hunter, / Tied by the rope, and swim by the water'; an old rhyme which was once said by children to others who had been mooching!

Mumble – to eat without appetite

Munge – to munch

Nuncheon or nunch – lunch

Panteny – pantry

Pethy – crumby, used to describe bread

Pifkin – a pipkin, little jug

Pig-meat – pork, not bacon

Pikelets – crumpets

Pith or peth – the crumb of bread

Posset – bread soaked in beer

Pot-fruit – the best fruit for eating

Proofy or pruffy – nourishing

Scrimmet – a small piece of meat

Scrump – to eat ravenously

Shotpot – a person who spent so much in an ale-house that they were entitled to the landlord's pot or shot flagon!

Siddow or zidder – soft, tender; used to describe peas that have become soft while being boiled

Skim dick – inferior home-made cheese

Skimmer lad – a flat dumpling made of dough boiled on a skimmer

Smalter – small beer

Snowl or snole – a lump of bread or cheese

Souring – vinegar

Spot – a drop or small quantity of drink

Squench – to quench

Tach or tack – an unpleasant flavour

Tack – stuff, usually said of food or drink, and in a negative sense

Tantadlin – apple dumpling

Taplash – bad, small beer

Thumb-piece – a piece of bread with meat or cheese held between the finger and thumb

Tiff – a small draught of liquor

Tip – a draught of liquor

Tosticated – intoxicated or puzzled

Tot – a small mug or tumbler holding about a quarter of a pint. They were generally given with a jug of beer, perhaps to eke it out for the maximum number of glasses!

Tud – an apple dumpling

Twer – small beer

Two-meal cheese – cheese which was made from the skimmed milk of the evening's meal, to which was added the new milk of the morning's meal

Vinney or vinnied – mouldy

Vlitchen – a flitch of bacon

Wallish – watery, poor; used to describe drinks such as cider

Home sweet home

Back-let – the back part of a house

Backside – the back of a house

Bad or bod – the green outer husks off walnuts

Bad or band – to take the husks off walnuts

Bake – to toast, of bread

Blacksmith's daughter – a lock or key to a door or gate, a padlock

Blatch – soot or dirt

Blatchy – black, dirty

Candle tinning – candle lighting, evening

Coal shute – coal scuttle

Cord – a measure of fire-wood, 4ft by 8ft by 3ft

Cooch and corner – nook and cranny

Courts – farm houses

Crane – a small iron frame fitted on the grate, to suspend pots, etc. from

Dinket – to dandle a baby

Dough kiver – the trough in which dough was made

Flannin – flannel

Flask – a basket

Flower knot – a flower bed

Gad-about – a device once used for teaching children to walk. It consisted of a large hoop on castors at the bottom, connected by a framework with a small hoop on top. The hoop circled the child under the arms, keeping it from falling, and allowing it plenty of space to move (or 'gad') about the room.

Lum – a chimney

Lewth – warmth, shelter

Lid – a cupboard door

Loothy – warm, snug

At your leisure

Backrackets – fireworks

Bandore – a violoncello or bassoon

Cruddle – to crouch up in a corner, nestle

Doppet – to play a musical instrument jerkily

Hoblionkers – a children's game played with horse chestnuts

Lop-lolly – a lazy fellow

Miche or mooche – to play truant

Nale – an ale-house

Olf – horseplay

Rushing – a game played with long narrow pins

Shinny – hockey

Tid – playful, frolicsome

Having fun at the Gloucester Mop Fair in 1910

pastandpresentpublications.com

Nature's world

Ails – beards of barley

Airsens – Hawthorn berries

Aps – aspen tree

Ash – the lilac

Ashen tree – the ash

Avels – barley beards

Aveller – a machine for dressing barley

Ay-grass – old pasture ground which has not been cropped by animals for a long time

Bean helms – bean stalks

Blow – blossom

Brit – to shell out; used to describe over-ripe corn shedding from the ear

Brittle – of the air, crisp

Boss – tuft of grass

Bottom – a valley

Brake – a copse

Brush or brash – small branches of trees used for pea sticks

Bullace – a wild plum

Bulls'-peats – a rough fibrous grass, very blunting to the scythe

Bulls'-polls – a kind of rough coarse grass that grows in tufts

Bushet – to throw out suckers, to shoot out at the roots, to sprout

Candlemas bells – the snowdrop

Canker – the dandelion

Catching – of the weather, uncertain

Casalty – changeable, uncertain of the weather

Chit – to sprout

Chizzom – to bud, sprout, germinate
Cleachers – the layers of a hedge
Knap – a knoll
Messengers – small detached clouds showing oncoming rain
Mirkshet or muckshet – twilight
Lipping or lippy – wet, rainy; a lippin' time means a wet season
Pen – hill

Continuing a long rural heritage iStock

People

Acquaintance – a sweetheart
Adone! – have done! Leave off!
Abear – to tolerate, endure
All about – in a state of confusion

All as is – all there is to be said

Allow – to reckon, consider

Aminded – disposed, inclined

Advocate – partiality, liking for

Afeard – frightened

Agree with – to put up with

Aground – on foot

A-hopping – fretting

Aim – to try, endeavour, intend

Ankley – ankle

Appear – appearance

Arg – to argue

Attern – fierce, cruel, ill-natured

Away with – to suffer, to put up with

Ax – to ask

Awhile – to find time for anything

Backfriend – a hang nail

Best – to get the better of a person, to cheat

Beteem – to indulge with

Back your fancy – to change your mind, alter your opinion

Baff – to stammer

Balderdash – abusive language

Banter about – to potter about

Banter down – to haggle, cheapen

Bandy – to get about, to knock about

Bather – to go hither and thither in quest of anything, to fuss after

Beeall – to abuse

Barney – a row, disturbance

Be'ant – am not, or not

Beest thee, thee beesn't – thou art, thou art not

Bellock – to bellow, roar

Bellows, bellers – used of the lungs and throat

Bellus – to hurry

Belt – to bustle about

Belver – to belch

Bide – to stay, to dwell, to remain

Big – to make big, magnify

Bist – you are

Blather – to talk indistinctly

Blob-mouthed – talkative

Boffle – to worry, perplex, annoy

Bofflement – a bother, state of perplexity

Bord – to prognosticate

Bost – to burst

Boxy – all square, all right, shipshape

Brevet – to hunt about, to pry

Breveting – gadding about, rummaging

Browsy – a ruddy complexion

Bruggle through – to struggle through a difficulty

Brave – well in health, strong in appearance

Breeds – the brim of a hat

Briched – well off

Brother-law – brother-in-law

Buff – to stammer

Buship – a bishop

Butty – a mate, work fellow

Byer – lonelier

Caddle – a row, fuss, bother, a muddle

Caddle – to make a bustle, fuss or bother, also to gossip or to do odd jobs

Caddlement – a bother, fuss

Caddling – trifling, gossiping, false

Cadge – to beg in an indirect way

Cagmag – to nag, irritate, to speak abusively

Cakers – the tonsils

Call one out of one's name – to call by a nickname

Candle of the eye – the pupil

Cant – to toss, throw, to gossip, to tell tales, to slander

Capital well – exceedingly well

Capper – head

Cark – care

Carneying – wheedling

Carryin's on – rude behaviour

Cawkey oaf – a touchy person

Cham – to chew

Chatterpie – a chatterbox

Chaun – to gape

Chaw – to chew

Chin cough – whooping cough

Chice – choice, particular, fastidious

Childer – children

Chock – to chuck, throw

Clip – to embrace

Clomber – to climb

Cracks – 'I can't tell no cracks of myself' – I can't give a very good account of my health

Craiky – weak, infirm, shaky

Comfortable – agreeable, pleasant, easy to get on with, of a person

Comical – out of sorts, very poorly

Collogue – to consult together

Conjobbe – to mend in a bungling manner

Crank – curious, odd

Crass – cantankerous, peevish

Curious – nice, dainty

Curst – ill-tempered/whimsical

Cust – sharp-witted

Fritchety – fretful, peevish, fidgety

Fussicky – fussy, fidgety

Gallus – mischievous, vicious, impudent, reckless

Gammut – sport, joke, mischief

Make – mate, companion, lover

Market peart – somewhat the worse for alcohol, as after a visit to the market!

Marriage lines – marriage certificate

Mazzard – the head or face

Megrums – whims, fancies

Mess over – to make a fuss over a child

Mimping – dainty

Misword – unpleasant words, disagreement

Momble – to muddle, confuse, perplex, also to tangle

Mugglement – a state of muddle, confusion

Nan – an expression which shows that the speaker does not hear or understand what has been said to them!

Neighbour – to gossip among neighbours

Nettlesome – quarrelsome

Niff – a quarrel, wrangle

Niggle – to nag, tease

Nither – to make grimaces at

Nogman – a stupid person

Noration – gossip

Not half saved – daft

Nottable – clever, famous

Nuncle – uncle

Oaf – to play the fool

Old – sly, cunning, suspicious

Owless – careless, lazy, thick-headed, devil-may-care.

Peart – bright, lively

Pearten up – to grow lively

Pick out – to find or worm out information

A Gloucester Coop milk delivery cart at the turn of the 20th century
Creative Commons

An honest day's work

A-chatting – picking up chats or small sticks

Arrest – harvest

Author – authority

Billy – the tray used for carrying iron ore

Billy-boy – the person who carries the 'billy'

Blow up – call to workmen to get back to work

Bout – in ploughing or sowing, one furrow up and one down

Bow-haul – to tow a vessel by manpower

Brandfire – bonfire

Brown crops – pulse crops, beans, peas, etc.

Bray – hay raked into long rows

Badger – a jobbing dealer in fruit, coal, etc. In the past, a person buying up butter in Gloucester butter market for the purpose of selling it again in the neighbouring markets was called a butter badger.

Bag – to bag peas is to cut them with a reaping hook with a long handle

Bailey – a farm bailiff

Bandy – a tool used for spreading cow dung in the fields

Barton – hay raked up in rows

Bar – a crow-bar

Barton or barken – a farmyard, also specifically 'the cow barton' – a yard with a shed

Boat – the barges which went up and down the Severn River with coal, hay, etc

Bolt – a truss of straw

Boltin' – a truss of straw weighing 24lbs

Bonds – twisted twigs for tying up faggots, beans, etc

Buckle – a twig pointed at both ends for securing thatch

Burl – an implement once used in cloth factories for picking knots and lint out of cloth

Burn – a burden of hay, wood, or straw

Burrow-hurdles – hurdles wattled with straw to protect ewes in lambing

Bury – a heap of roots or potatoes covered up with earth, or a rabbit hole

Butter kiver – a tub for washing newly-made butter

Butty man – a sub-contractor in a colliery

Carter – waggoner

Carr – to carry

Cast – to yield, of crops

Char or chir – a job

Clay-stone – blue and white limestone once used for lime burning

Clinching net – a bag net once used for fishing

Cod – the middle part of the blade of a reaping or hedging hook, or of a sickle

Come here – call to a cart horse to bear to the left

Cratch – a rack for hay, etc; also the rack at the back of a carrier's cart

Daak – to dig up weeds

Dey-house – the dairy

Feneague or fernaigue – to shirk, play truant

Friggling – loitering or trifling about work

Hag – a job

Hit – an abundant crop of fruit

Jog, jogget or jobbut – a small load or burden of hay, etc.

Jopple – a little job

Kerd or kyerd – to card wool

Laiking – idling, playing truant

Leer – horses which were harnessed, but drawing nothing were called leer horses. The leer waggon was the spare wagon of three used in carting hay.

Lent grain – the spring crops

Lighting stock – steps for mounting or dismounting from a horse

Lug – a long stick used for knocking down apples

Mawkin – a scarecrow

Meer – a strip of grass or ridge left as a boundary in common fields

Morin' axe – a two-edged axe for cutting the roots of trees

Mouster – to clear out, e.g. to clear out a wasps' nest or to clear beasts out of a field

Nager – to work laboriously or clumsily

Outride – a commercial traveller

Owner – a title given to the proprietor of a boat or trow

Pargeter – a plasterer

Peck – a pickaxe

Pick – a hay fork

Rickmould – an old trick which used to be played on new workers in the fields was that they would be sent to fetch 'the rickmould' from a long way away and would return with a heavy weight in a sack!

Scowl of brow – judging by the eye instead of by measurement

Scowles – the sides of workings in coal or iron mines falling in

Excerpts from *A Glossary of Dialect and Archaic Words Used in the County of Gloucester* by JOHN DRUMMOND ROBERTSON, published 1890

Can you speak 'Vurrist'?

The Forest of Dean iStock

The Forest of Dean, which lies in the western part of Gloucestershire, is special for many reasons. Not only does it cover an area as big as 24,000 acres, it is also located right between the River Severn and the River Wye. This isolation from the rest of the country is probably why it has such a strong identity, including its own dialect. The Forest of Dean had a long tradition of jobs in industries such as forestry and mining. It is one of the few remaining ancient forests in England and is the largest oak forest in England. The area is known for having inspired writers such as DENNIS POTTER, J.K. ROWLING and J.R.R. TOLKIEN.

'It is a rich and very heavily flavoured mixture of the speed and lilt of the Welsh borderland, the broad, lengthened vowel sounds and buttery emphases of the West Country and many distinctive local words and rhythms of its own.'

DENNIS POTTER, speaking about the Forest of Dean dialect in 1962

J.K. Rowling iStock

A'n't – have not

Agwain – going

Aim – think, suppose, reckon: 'I d'aim', expect

Aisne – small wood

Arle – alder

Astn't – hast not

Bait – food

Bannut – walnut

Bathered out – tired

Bist – to be

Bistn't – are you not

Black lead – graphite

Boy-chap – young man

Breadtime – mid-morning meal

Brevetting – wandering about

Browst – twigs

Chops – mouth

Chup – cheap

Clane – clean

Clate off – clear off

Coleford collar – scarf

Comp – candle

Cordwood – wood for stacking

Cyawpsin' – too talkative

Daggled – exhausted, tired

Dipple – pit entered down steep slope

Drow – throw

Elba – elbow

Ern – either

Ettles – nettles

Feythur – father

Flump – fall down

Frail – a small canvas bag

Gale – area of ground for which a miner has mineral rights

Gaust – gorse

Gurt – great, big

Gyule – sneer

Hain – to enclose, as when part of a forest is enclosed

Jadder – liar

Jasper – wasp

Lomber – to climb with difficulty

Lug pole – pole for shaking down cider apples or perry pears

Meend – a village common or green

Mommuck – a mess

Mullockin' – lazing

Nithered – cold, frozen

Ockerd – awkward

Oik – lift, throw

Ood – wood

Oont – mole

Phizog – face

Putcheons or putts – cone-shaped baskets used to catch salmon

Quist – wood pigeon

Quomp – to stop

Rinnuck – small pig in litter

Sawney – soft, daft

Ship badger – a person who tends sheep

Sprack – lively

Squap – to tread or lean unevenly

Squit, squitter – nonsense

Stunnem – a very strong type of cider which used to be popular in the Forest!

Tanglefoot – cider

Tats – Forest or Welsh sheep

Tith – teeth

Tripe hound – silly person

Tudjamler – tadpole

Tump – a barrow or hill

Tushin' – carrying

Vark – fork

Vella – fellow

Vetch – fetch

Vire – fire

Vorest – forest

Wapper – wasp

Wiffle – stink

Wum – home
Wurrut – worry
Yalla – yellow
Yud – head
Zarve – serve

Gloucestershire sayings

Of bad singing – *'I'd as zoon 'ear a raek [rake] and basket.'*
Of a useless article – *'It's as handy as a twud wi' side pockuts.'*
Of a ne'er-do-well – *'There's a shabby zhip [i.e, a sheep with scab] in every vlock.'*
Of a knowing boy – *'Ee's as artful as an old man ninety.'*
Of activity – *'As busy as a cat in a tripe shop.'*
Of laziness – *'He was born tired.'*
Of an indistinct voice – *'Like a dumbledore in a pitcher.'*
Of doing something futile or useless – *'What's the good of 'ees throwin' straws at the wind?'*
Of a person who leaves dirty work to others – *'He makes the bullets, and leaves we to shoot them.'*
'No carrion will kill a crow.'
'He's as hard as a wood pile twoad.'
'As hardy as a Vorest peg.'
'It do come as nat'ral as hooping do to owls.'
'Dost look as handy wi' that as a pig do wi' a musket.'

'From Christmas-tide to New 'us tide,
The days do get a cock's stride;
From New 'us tide to Candlemas tide,
The days do get an hour wide.'

Cobbler's Creed Monday is a Saint's day;
Tuesday's just another such a day;
Wednesday's the middle pin;
Thursday's too late to begin;
Friday we must fast and pray;
Saturday never was but half a day.'

'Saturday new, and Sunday full,
It allus rines [rains], and it allus ool [will].

'Rain on Good Friday and Easter Day,
Brings plenty of grass but little good hay.'

The following grammatical peculiarities are worth noting:

In names of places, the genitive case is invariably employed, as
Littledean's Hill, Over's Bridge, Highnam's Church, Stroud's
Water. With verbs denoting attitude, the past instead of the present
participle is used after the auxiliary was; thus, 'he was stood in the
road,' 'he was leant against the wall', 'he was sat on the chair'.

Excerpts from *A Glossary of Dialect and Archaic Words Used in the County of Gloucester* by JOHN DRUMMOND ROBERTSON, published 1890

Sayings from the Cotswolds

Lower Slaughter iStock

'A copy of your coimtenance' – being deceptive

'All manner' – a phrase which was once used to express all kinds of annoyance, mainly to describe the behaviour of a person who is intrusive and inconsiderate!

'All's one for that' – Notwithstanding your objection, the case remains the same

'King' – a common way of making a favourable comparison was to say that one thing is a king to something else

'Limb' – used to describe anything which causes trouble!

'Drap it, drap it!' – Drop it!

'Gallows bad', 'Gallows drunk,' 'a Gallows cheat' – pronounced 'Gallus' – 'bad enough for the gallows'

'Hand over head' – used to express anything done in haste or disorder

'I cannot away with' – I can't forget about it, I can't bear it

'I'll tell you what' – I'll give you my opinion or decision on this topic

'It'll come right aater a bit' – this difficulty will pass

'Month's mind' – a mind unsettled on any particular plan

'Next of kin' – in relation to, rather than related to; e.g. a glove – next of kin to the hand

'Overseen' and 'overlooked' – bewitched or led astray by an evil influence

'Play the bear' or 'Play the very Buggan with you' – to spoil, to harass; 'Buggan' referred to Satan or any other malign spirit!

'Quite natural' – anything done easily, as a matter of course

'To and again' – to move backwards and forwards, to go to a certain point and to return again

'You'll meet with it' – a threat that punishment will follow the course a person is pursuing

'Whatever' frequently ends a sentence prematurely, the words 'may happen' or 'by any means' being struck off. It is mostly used negatively, as 'I would not do it – whatever.' 'He would not help himself – whatever.' This phrase, in spite of the ludicrous effect which attends it, is sometimes heard in the better walks of life in the Cotswolds.

The habit, however, of substituting the word 'Aunt' for 'Grandmother,' which is very common in this district, deserves consideration

Excerpts from *A Glossary of the Cotswold, Gloucestershire, Dialect* by RICHARD WEBSTER HUNTLEY, published 1868

'You are a man of Duresley' – Used to one who has broken his promise; and probably alluded to an ancient and notorious breach of faith, by some inhabitants of that town, the particulars of which are now forgotten

'It's as long coming as Cotswould barley' – This is applied to such things as are slow but sure. The corn in this cold country, on the Woulds, exposed to the winds, bleak and shelterless, is very backward at the first, but afterwards overtakes the forwardest in the county; if not in the barn in the bushel, both for quantity and goodness thereof.

'A Cotswould Lion' – That is a sheep, Cotswould being famous for its sheepwalks or pastures.

'He looks (or seems) as if he had lived on Tewksbury mustard' – Said of any peevish or snappish person, or one having a cross, fierce or ill-natured countenance. Tewkesbury is a market-town in this county, famous for its mustard, which is extremely hot, biting, and poignant; and therefore, by this proverb, supposed to communicate those qualities, to persons fed with it.

Excerpts from *A Provincial Glossary; with a Collection of local Proverbs, and Popular Superstitions* by FRANCIS GROSE, published 1811

George Ridler's Oven

Folk songs can hold fascinating secrets about a place's past, and none more so than the Gloucestershire folk song, *George Ridler's Oven*. An 18th-century book reveals some of the story below:

It is now generally understood that the words of this song have a hidden meaning, which was only known to the members of the Gloucestershire Society, whose foundation dates from the year 1657. This was three years before the restoration of Charles II and when the people were growing weary of the rule of Oliver Cromwell. The Society consisted of Loyalists, whose object in combining was to be prepared to aid in the restoration of the ancient constitution of the kingdom whenever a favourable opportunity should present itself. The Cavalier or Royalist party were supported by the Roman

Catholics of the old and influential families of the kingdom; and some of the Dissenters, who were disgusted with the treatment they received from Cromwell, occasionally lent them a kind of passive aid. Taking these considerations as the key note to the song, attempts have been made to discover the meaning which was originally attached to its leading words.

Excerpt from *Legends, Tales, and Songs, in the Dialect of the Peasantry of Gloucestershire*

So was the song simply gobbledegook or secret Royalist propaganda? The theories suggest that George Ridler symbolises King Charles I, the 'oven' was the Cavalier party and the 'stwons' that 'built the oven', and that 'came out of the Bleakney's Quar', refers to the followers of the Marquis of Worcester, alongside other hidden meanings! The Gloucestershire Society, which has sung the song every year for many years, states:

"It has been believed for nearly two centuries that the Gloucestershire Society, an ancient county charity, began life as a secret Royalist cell, immediately following the English Civil War. Recent research has shown that the song 'George Ridler's Oven' is in fact an amalgam of three popular folk-songs, which did not exist as a single entity at the time the Society was formed".

You can read about the theories behind the song on the website of the Gloucestershire Society at **www. gloucestershiresociety.org.uk/The-Secrets-of-George-Ridler-s-Oven/the-secrets-of-george-ridler-s-oven.html.** We'll probably never know the complete truth behind George Ridler's Oven, but one thing is for sure: this folk song is a fascinating aspect of Gloucestershire's history!

George Ridler's Oven

The Stwons that built George Ridler's Oven,
And thauy keum from the Bleakeney's Ouar;
And George he wur a Jolly old Mon,
And his Yead it graw'd above his Yare.

One thing of George Ridler I must commend,
And that wur vor a notable Theng:
He meud his Braags avore he died
Wi' any dree Brothers his Zons zhou'd zeng.

Thers's Dick the Treble and John the Mean
(Let every Mon zing in his auwn Pleace),
And George he wur the elder brother,
And therevore he would zing the Beass.

Mine Hostess's Moid (and her Neaum t'wur Nell),
A pretty Wench, and I lov'd her well;
I lov'd her well, good Reauzon why,
Becase zshe lov'd my Dog and I.

Excerpts from *Legends, Tales, and Songs, in the Dialect of the Peasantry of Gloucestershire*

Gloucestershire in the written word

The world of Gloucestershire has been captured in a number of books about growing up in the area. The first is the idyllic *Cider with Rosie* by LAURIE LEE. Published in 1959, it is an account of the author's childhood in Slad, Gloucestershire shortly after the end of World War I. It is part of a trilogy and has sold over six million copies throughout the world. Another book which has brought part of Gloucestershire to life is *A Child in the Forest* by WINIFRED FOLEY. This autobiographical book tells the story of Foley's childhood in the Forest of Dean. Recognised for having drawn public attention to the Forest, the book has since been renamed *Full Hearts and Empty Bellies*. Having started out as a handwritten project submitted to a professor of social history, the book went on to be serialised on BBC Radio 4's *Woman's Hour* in 1973! Less famous, perhaps, but no less critically acclaimed is the TV play, *Blue Remembered Hills* by DENNIS POTTER. This tells the story of children in the

Forest of Dean during the Second World War. It was first shown in 1979, with the most noticeable aspect of it being that while the characters are children, they are played by adults. Another important aspect of the play is that the characters speak in the Forest of Dean dialect. Potter's characters talk in this dialect in other works such as *The Singing Detective* and *Pennies from Heaven*. This is no surprise when you consider that Dennis Potter was the eldest son of a coal miner in the Forest of Dean. It's even less surprising when you consider how strongly Potter felt about his local area, once describing it as 'this heart-shaped land'. He also writes detailed accounts of life in the Forest of Dean in his books, *The Glittering Coffin* and *The Changing Forest: Life in the Forest of Dean Today*. Two of Potter's earliest television plays, *Blue Remembered Hills* and *The Beast with Two Backs*, were filmed on location in the Forest.

> *It just so happens that the Forest of Dean being green and hilly and grey and rearing up between two rivers and the dialect was 'thee' and 'thou' like in the King James Bible. It was perfectly natural to speak 'thee', 'thou' like in the King James Bible. It was perfectly natural to speak 'thee', 'thou', and the more tenderly you felt the more certainly you would use – I mean my father would always say 'Is't thou alright, old butty?' if it was a kindly question: 'Are you all right?'*

DENNIS POTTER, in an interview with JOHN COOK in 1990

The Forest Poetess

Long before writers like Potter and Lee brought the Forest of Dean alive for a fascinated public, the Forest Poetess was capturing it in words. Born in 1784, CATHERINE DREW wrote many poems about the forest. Sadly, while some of these were published in 1841 in a book, A Collection of Poems on the Forest of Dean and its Neighbourhood, just 100 copies of the book were printed! Fortunately, Drew's reputation as a poet in the area survived. Her forest beginnings are summed up in one of her poems:

The Forest of Dean iStock

In a little thatched cottage, as free as a King,
Near a green shady grove, where the birds used to sing
I was born and was bred, in the Forest of Dean,
I knew nothing of town or what it did mean.

It is believed that Drew had a fairly tough life, not least because she had eight children. She is now celebrated with a memorial in the churchyard of St. John the Evangelist Church in Cinderford.

The Laureate of Gloucestershire

As you might guess for a person dubbed the **Laureate of Gloucestershire**, F.W. HARVEY's poetry was hugely popular in his day. Frederick William Harvey is remembered as much for his poetry as for his acts of bravery during the Great War, when he was captured and attempted daring escapes. His poem *Ducks* was featured in the BBC's *The Nation's 100 Favourite Poems*. Another epithet applied to Harvey was 'The Forest Poet'. This was because he was brought up in Minsterworth (after being born in Hartpury). When Harvey was a pupil at The King's School in Gloucester, he formed a close friendship with IVOR GURNEY, who would go on to be one of the great First World War Poets. Harvey and Gurney also became friends with the Gloucestershire composer HERBERT HOWELLS, who set a number of Harvey's poems to music.

The war was a major influence on Harvey's writing, along with his rural roots. Having enlisted in the 5th Battalion Gloucestershire Regiment, Harvey began to write to entertain his fellow soldiers, with pieces in the *5th Gloucester Gazette*, the newspaper produced by the battalion's chaplain. He published his first book of poems, *A Gloucestershire Lad At Home and Abroad*, in 1916, the same year he was captured by the Germans while on a mission. This captivity inspired

Harvey to write more, and he was even able to send his work back to England to be published! Harvey's longing to return to Gloucestershire can be heard vividly in his poem, *In Flanders*, where he writes:

I'm homesick for my hills again –
To see above the Severn plain
Unscabbarded against the sky
The blue high blade of Cotswold lie.

Harvey's most famous poem was inspired by an image drawn by a fellow prisoner – of ducks. This poem is regularly featured in poetry anthologies, but Harvey is also recognised for poems such as *The Horses, Spring 1924, That Catch* and *If We Return*. Harvey worked as a defence solicitor after the war, but then moved into radio broadcasting. Thanks to his confidence in speaking and a natural talent for mimicking others, he enjoyed a long-lasting career before his death in 1957.

Another chapter

A fitting final chapter to the story of the Laureate of Gloucestershire came with the news that in 2013, an unpublished novel was discovered among Harvey's papers at his former home in Gloucestershire, following his son's death. Parts of the novel were first found in a brown envelope in a garage! The novel is called *Will Harvey: A*

Romance and follows the story of two brothers all the way from their schooldays to the trenches. The novel, which explores the impact of war on young lives, has been called 'a jewel of a find'.

Ivor Gurney

Another Gloucestershire native is recognised as being one of the most important voices of wartime poetry. Born in 1890, not only was IVOR GURNEY a poet, he was also a composer. Gurney wrote no fewer than two hundred songs, more than three hundred poems and verse pieces and a number of chamber and instrumental works. Maybe surprisingly considering his combined musical and poetic talents, he set only a small number of his own poems to music. Probably his most well-known work is *Severn Meadows* while his best-known compositions include his Five Elizabethan Songs and the song-cycles *Ludlow and Teme* and *The Western Playland*.

Sadly, while Gurney had hoped that the structure of army life would allow him to cope more easily with the mental health issues that afflicted him, he ended his days in an asylum. Yet it was during his 15 years in the asylum that he crafted poetry powerfully expressing the experience of being a soldier. Gurney's legacy was recognised when he went on to become one of 16 poets of the Great War commemorated on a slate stone in Westminster Abbey's Poet's Corner. Another moving memorial to Gurney can be found near Ypres, close to where he became the victim of a mustard gas attack in 1917. You can also find a blue plaque celebrating his life and achievements on Eastgate Street in Gloucester.

The Cotswold Poet

FRANK MANSELL became known as 'the Cotswold Poet' after the positive reception to his compilation of poems, *Cotswold Ballads*, in 1969. Mansell was born in London, but came from a long line of Cotswold farmers. He fitted writing poetry around his full-time job in the engineering section of the GPO. His poems were frequently featured in the local press and he gave regular readings of his work. Mansell also found time to take an active part in village cricket and to pursue his passion for astrology! He became great friends with writer Laurie Lee almost immediately after they met in the pub at Slad. It was with Lee's support that Mansell published his first collection of poems. Lee summed up the power of Mansell's poetry in the foreword he wrote for his book of poems:

> *The poet's voice reverberates with the resonance of the Cotswold Highlands, with all the smooth wrapped hardness of moss-dressed stone...*

From Tennyson to Jilly Cooper

Gloucestershire has inspired an array of writers, in many genres. You don't have to look very hard in your local bookshop to discover the works of the authors who have made the county their setting or their home! Well-known romance writer and journalist **JILLY COOPER** lives near Stroud. Her achievements in entertaining readers with her rather naughty books have been recognised with an Honorary Doctorate of Letters from the University of Gloucestershire!

> *'What is this life if, full of care,*
> *We have no time to stand and stare.*

These words have brought perspective to many people since they were first written by poet and self-described 'supertramp', **W.H. DAVIES**. Born in Wales in 1871, Davies forged an extraordinary life for himself after hitch-hiking across North America and having countless adventures. The lines above from his poem Leisure are quoted in a stone plaque over the front door of Glendower, the cottage in Nailsworth which Davies made his home until he died.

Author **SUSAN HILL** has been enthralling readers with books such as *The Woman in Black*, *A Bit of Singing and Dancing* and *I'm the King of the Castle* for many years. While she was born in Scarborough, Hill now lives a farmhouse in rural Gloucestershire from where she runs her own small publishing company, Long Barn Books.

ALFRED, LORD TENNYSON, one of the world's best-known and best-loved poets, has a strong association with Gloucestershire, even though he was born in Lincolnshire. The man who went on to be the longest serving Poet Laureate of Great Britain and Ireland lived in Cheltenham from 1846 to 1850 after he was left with no money following a failed business venture involving woodcarving machinery! He made the move for health reasons, to take Cheltenham's famous waters. It is thought that Tennyson wrote some of his most important works while he was living in Cheltenham, including most of In Memoriam.

JOANNA TROLLOPE OBE is the author of many highly acclaimed novels. She was born in Minchinhampton and once said about the place that 'Being born somewhere with a strong local sense, like the Cotswolds, gave me not just a sense of rootedness, but a capacity to value landscape and weather and the rich life of smallish communities.'

Gloucestershire Harvest Home Choruses

No. I.

Here's a health unto our master,
The founder of the feast;
I hope to God wi' all my heart
His soul in Heav'n may rest!
That all his works may prosper
Whatever he takes in hand;
For we are all his servants
And all at his command!

No. II.

Here's a health unto our mistress,
The best of one and twenty;
Heigh-ho, is it so, is it so ? It is so!
Fill it up a little fuller, for I think it looks quite empty,
And down let it go, let it let it go!
And if you drink too deep
You can go to bed and sleep,
And drive away sorrow and woe.

No. III.

Here's a health to the man this house do belong,
For providing of us this good cheer;
Here's health to his wife all the days of her life,

Lord send him good crops for next year.
And prosper his flock, and all his whole stock,
His family well to maintain;
Then take up this cup and drink it all up,
For there's plenty to fill it again.

Excerpts from *Legends, Tales, and Songs, in the Dialect of the Peasantry of Gloucestershire*

Speaking Gloucestershire in the South Pacific

You can travel 12,000 miles and still hear the Gloucestershire accent – to the South Pacific, to be precise! This is because the residents of the very smallest of the Cook Islands speak with a Gloucestershire accent. It's all thanks to one man, according to the Daily Mail, that the people of Palmerston Island, are all descendants of William Marsters, a carpenter from Bibury who settled in the South Pacific back in 1863. Now all 63 of the island's residents speak with a Gloucestershire accent and researchers are trying to find out more about this fascinating link between the South Pacific and Gloucestershire!

Gloucestershire in sayings

'Scratch Gloucestershire and find Rome'

Part of the old hypocaust or heating system at Chedworth Roman Villa in the Cotswolds iStock

This is said to be an old Gloucestershire saying expressing the richness of the county's Roman roots. It's no wonder that the people of the past used to say this, considering how packed Gloucestershire is with Roman remains! In fact, the city of Gloucester first began as a Roman town. In AD 64, the Romans built a new fort on the site of Gloucester town centre. While they moved on in around AD 75, the site of the fort was turned into a town for retired soldiers and went on to be known as Glevum by the Romans. These days, you can still very much scratch Gloucestershire and see its Roman past in places such as Chedworth Roman Villa, Lydney Park Roman Camp and, of course, Gloucester itself.

'As sure as God's in Gloucestershire'

As you can probably guess, this old proverb makes a clear statement about the county's religious past. It certainly has a rich religious history. Christianity was officially accepted in Britain in AD 170 under Good King Lucius, who built the church of St Mary de Lode in Gloucester. It is also said that there is a tree in a churchyard in Gloucester which is a direct descendant of the one on which Judas Iscariot hanged himself. Here are two older definitions of the saying:

'Thie Proverb is said to have its Rise, on Account that there were more rich and mitred Abbies in that, than in any two Shires in England besides; but some from William of Malmsbury refer it to the Fruitfulness of it in Religion, in that it is said to have returned the Seed of the Gospel with the Increase of an hundred fold.'

Excerpt from *Divers Proverbs with Their Explication and Illustration* by NATHAN BAILEY, published 1917

A saying originating from the number and riches of the religious houses in this county; said to be double in number and value to those founded in any other in England.

Excerpts from *A Provincial Glossary; with a Collection of Local Proverbs, and Popular Superstitions* by FRANCS GROSE, published 1811

The place names of the Cotswolds

Chipping Campden iStock

You can learn a lot about a place by exploring its place names, especially when they are as packed full of history as the Cotswolds! When it comes to the name *'the Cotswolds'*, one belief is that the word *'wolds'* is derived from an ancient English word which means *'gentle hills'*, so the name in fact combines two English words: *wold* together with *cots*, referring to sheep enclosures. Another view along the same lines is that the name Cotswolds comes from *'sheep shelters'* *(cots) 'in rolling hills' (wolds)*. If you look more closely at many

52

of the evocative place names in the Cotswolds, you'll find even more fascinating links to the past. This is because so many of the names are based on Old English ones. Take the word *'Chipping'*, featured in place names like Chipping Norton and Chipping Sodbury. The word is actually based on an Old English word which means *'market'*! So Chipping Norton essentially means *'market town north'*, though it is affectionately referred to by locals as *'Chippy'!* Another interesting fact about place names in the area is that, despite its harsh-sounding name, Upper Slaughter was given the epithet *'the sainted village'* because none of its residents who went to fight died in World War I. If someone says you should see the *'Venice of the Cotswolds'*, you need to head for Bourton-on-the-Water. It's the most visited village in the area.

A Gloucestershire Zong o Zocial Science

Your sarvant, my betters in station and wealth,
And thank 'ee fur drinkun the labourer's health;
And, Zur, I can't tell you how grateful we be
For the good advice you've a bin givun to we.

'Tis true, my grand friends, as afore me I finds,
There's nothun like rubbun together our minds;
For zo we both taches and larns zummat new
And now let me zay just a few words to you.

Bourton-on-the-Water Andy & Susan Caffrey

Extravagunce I bean't afeard to spake plain
To the shrewd higher ranks is the gentlevolks bane.
What lots of you workun men falls a prey
To that sad love o' yourn for show-off and display.

No doubt you doan't spend all your incomes in beer,
But what do your house-rents, now, come to a year?
Eight hundred, a thousand and moor, I be told,
And by-n-by the furnitur comes to be zold.

There's likewise your footmen in all zarts o' plush,
Bedizened enough to make e'er a man blush;
Wi' the hair o' their heads full o' powder an' grease;
My friends, this here nonsense 'tis time vor to zease.

Excerpt from *Legends, Tales, and Songs, in the Dialect of the Peasantry of Gloucestershire*

A folk heritage

George Ridler's Oven is not the only Gloucestershire folk song with a fascinating history. Two popular Christmas songs, *The Gloucestershire Wassail* and *The Holly and the Ivy*, also originated in Gloucestershire!

The Holly and the Ivy

This popular Christmas carol is believed to have pagan origins, while its words date right back to the 17th century.

Thought to have originated in the Cotswolds, the carol was first published in a broadside in 1710. In the mid-1800s, it was featured in a collection of carols after the editor of the book heard it sung by a woman in Chipping Campden, and this was when its popularity really took off.

The Gloucestershire Wassail

Wassail! wassail! all over the town,
Our toast it is white and our ale it is brown;
Our bowl it is made of the white maple tree;
With the wassailing bowl, we'll drink to thee.

Here's to our horse, and to his right ear,
God send our master a happy new year:
A happy new year as e'er he did see,
With my wassailing bowl I drink to thee.

Excerpt from a version of *The Gloucestershire Wassail*

This song is believed to date all the way back to the Middle Ages, but was only published in 1928 in the Oxford Book of Carols. A wassail is essentially a kind of toast. The word is derived from an Old English greeting, waes hael, which means *'be healthy'!* When you toasted someone with these words, they would reply *drinc hael*. When people went *'wassailing'*, they would visit each house in their local area at Christmas, singing their local version of the Wassail

Song while carrying the *'wassail bowl'*. The bowl, which was frequently decorated with ribbons, was occasionally used to collect money or to hold drink, but was usually just a token decoration. The wassailing tradition was first recorded in Gloucestershire in the early 19th century and is believed to have continued in the area until as recently as the 1960s. Wassailing has actually started to make a comeback in Gloucestershire and elsewhere, linked to the resurgence of interest in folk music. It is interesting to note that there are many variations of The Gloucestershire Wassail, with the song differing from village to village.

A slice of Gloucester heritage

One type of food quite literally puts Gloucester in front of people across the world. This is of course cheese, whether you're a fan of the **Single Gloucester** or the **Double Gloucester variety**. According to the British Cheese Board:

'As early as 1498 so much cheese was being made in Gloucester that a permanent market was set up in Eastgate Street in the City of Gloucester. By Tudor times cow's milk was the norm across the Vale of Berkeley and down to Bristol. This came mainly from Old Gloucester cows whose milk was ideal for cheesemaking with small fat globules that made a fine even-textured cheese. In 1745 cattle plague all but wiped out the breed and it was

replaced by the Longhorn. Once re-stocked, farms began to supply more liquid milk into London. In 1789 production of Gloucester cheese was estimated at more than 1,000 tonnes.'

Source: The British Cheese Board

While **Double Gloucester** was considered the 'big cheese' and exported out of the county, **Single Gloucester** was enjoyed locally!

Why 'single' and 'double'?

Wondering what lies behind the names of the two types of Gloucester cheese? Well, there is no definitive answer. You can choose from:

REASON 1. Cream from the morning milk was added to the evening milk.

REASON 2. The milk had to be skimmed twice to make the double variety.

REASON 3. A Double Gloucester cheese is usually around twice the height of a Single Gloucester.

Whatever lies behind the names, the world continues to enjoy both types of Gloucester cheese to this day! Double Gloucester cheese plays a crucial part in one of Gloucestershire's best-known customs – the **Cooper's Hill Cheese-Rolling and Wake**. This annual event takes place at Cooper's Hill near Gloucester. The cheese featured in the tradition is a seven-to-nine-pound creation covered with a wooden casing to protect it during its journey down an extremely steep hill! This was once just a custom for the locals of Brockworth dating all the way back to the 15th century, but it is now attended by people from all over the world! While some believe that the cheese-rolling custom was originally connected with keeping up grazing rights to the common, another view is that it harks back to a pagan custom in which small bundles of burning brushwood were rolled down the hill to symbolise the start of the New Year. Either way, chasing a Double Gloucester cheese downhill continues to be popular to this day, though the custom is not without its controversies!

The Moolberry Tree

Twere in the merry month of May,
The birds wur singin on the le-e-e-ea,
When fust I zaw the lovely Molly
Oonder ne'uth the Moolberry Tree.

I axed her if she would be trew,
'Oh, 'ees I 'ool,' zays she to me;
A piece of goold we broke in two,
Onder ne'uth the Moolberry Tree.

T'were on a dark Dezember night
When Molly went across the Moor,
The znow coomd down and hid the light
An' Molly missed the cottage door.

Excerpt from *Legends, Tales, and Songs, in the Dialect of the Peasantry of Gloucestershire*

What is Gloucester Day?

The day named after Gloucester is, as you would probably guess, all about celebrating the history and culture of Gloucester! Taking place on or near 5 September, **Gloucester Day** specifically marks the lifting of the Siege of Gloucester in 1643 during the First English Civil War. During this important time for the city and the county as a whole, the people of Gloucester resisted the attacks of the Royalists. Their success in achieving this and in seeing the end of the siege was once an annual tradition and was the reason Gloucester was known as *'The City saved by God'*. This is because, during the conflict, the city's south gate was seriously damaged by cannon fire, then later collapsed, but was rebuilt in 1644 with the inscription: *A City Assaulted by Man, but Saved by God*. While local people stopped celebrating Gloucester Day in the 19th century, it was reinstated in 2009 and is now marked again with parades and all kinds of other events.

Cheltenham: a view from the past

Poultry and cattle are not among the least of the good things which the vicinity of Cheltenham affords: the excellence of the mutton is universally allowed. The hospitable host will frequently regale his visitor with Coteswold mutton; and, while the cup circulates freely, will bestow a panegyric on it, which exalts it to the rank of venison. The Egyptians of old could not more have reverenced their Ibis, than a thorough-bred Glocestershire farmer does a Coteswold sheep.

Cheltenham Spa

This Medicinal Spring, so justly celebrated for its numberless virtues, and so constantly attended by all ranks and descriptions of persons, was first known in 1716; but to what accident the discovery of it may be attributed, it is now, perhaps, too late to inquire. Some say that flocks of pigeons daily coming towards the spring, to feed on the salt which it left behind towards its source, induced Mr. Mason, the then proprietor of the ground, to take particular notice of it; when it was further remarked, that in hard frosty weather, when other springs were fast bound, this alone continued fluid. We call this emphatically The Spring, without addition or distinction, as being the original.

This water were first shewn on a horse grazing there; who by drinking at this place, and rolling himself in the grass where the spring oozed out, was cured of a violent humour and other disorders which he laboured under. Whether this is a fact or not, it has long been a custom for gentlemen to give it to their horses that have any humours; they drink it very willingly, and usually receive benefit from it.

The spring was in a meadow, a few furlongs distant from the town, on the south side, about six feet beneath the surface of the ground. The ground was originally the property of Mr. Higgs, of Sandford; but not knowing of a medicinal spring on the spot, he sold it with the adjoining land, in 1716, to Mr. Mason, who discovered the spring, which, for some time after its discovery, was open, and the people of the town and neighbourhood drank of it. In the year 1718, it was railed in, locked up, and a little shed thrown over it.

The first analysis of the water was made by Drs. Greville and Baird, soon after; and, in consequence of the good opinion resulting from such medical authority, its virtues became more generally known: it was, therefore, sold as a medicine, till the year 1721 when the well was let to Mr. Spencer, at 61l. per annum.

Excerpts from *The History of Cheltenham, and Account of its Environs*, by THOMAS FROGNALL DIBDIN and H. RUFF, published 1803

A woolly past

Wool. It may not sound like the most exciting thing in the world, but if it wasn't for wool, Gloucestershire wouldn't be the place it is today. It is thanks to the wool trade of the past that the county boasts so many stunning buildings. In the 12th century, people would say: '*In Europe the best wool is English and in England the best wool is Cotswold.*'

In the Middle Ages, the Cotswolds was well known as the source of some of the world's best wool. At that time, no less than half of England's economy was based around wool! This is all thanks to the growth of wool processing (or fulling, in which the cloth was thickened to make it warmer and more weatherproof), which grew from rural beginnings to become an important presence in large towns like Gloucester. The industry continued to grow, though not without some serious challenges in the 17th century. The coming of the Industrial Revolution brought new opportunities and problems for the industry in the area. If you visit Bibury, you can't miss the famously picturesque Arlington Row. Pretty it may be, but this line of cottages was originally built in 1380 as a monastic wool store, then turned into a row of weavers' cottages in the 17th century.

When is a lion not a lion?

When is a lion not a lion? When it is one of a rare breed of sheep from the Cotswolds! People once used to refer to the *'Cotswold Lion'*. which was in fact a type of local sheep. This traditional Cotswolds sheep with its beautiful long, golden-coloured fleece (referred to in the past as 'the golden fleece') was a crucial part of the success of Cotswolds wool across the world. Local monasteries and abbeys tended large flocks of these 'lions'. When the medieval wool trade was at its peak, it is thought that around 500,000 Cotswold Lions grazed on local hills! While it is believed by some that the lions owe their presence in the area to the Romans, others are firmly of the view that they have always existed in the Cotswolds.

In 1610, WILLIAM CAMDEN wrote in Britannia, his historical survey of Great Britain:

> *'In these Woulds there feed in great numbers, flockes of sheepe long necked and square of bulke and bone, by reason (as it is commonly thought) of the weally and hilly situation of their pasturage; whose wool being so fine and soft is had in passing great account among all nations.'*

Despite its contribution to the area and to the country as a whole, the Cotswold Lion almost became extinct in more recent years. Thankfully, while today it is classed as a rare breed, the Cotswold Lion is still very much alive.

From Gloucester to America

Did you know that a song sung by millions of Americans every year owes its identity in part to a connection with Gloucester? You probably wouldn't expect Gloucester to have a link with the US national anthem, *The Star-Spangled Banner*, but it does. The song, which is known as *The Anacreontic Song*, is set to the tune of a song called *To Anacraeon in Heaven*, written by JOHN STAFFORD-SMITH, who was baptised and buried at Gloucester Cathedral! Another surprising fact about this tune is that it was originally written for a gentlemen's social club in London. It was only later that it became popular in the USA, with lyrics from a poem by FRANCIS SCOTT KEY being set to the music. Another odd fact about the tune of *The Star-Spangled Banner* is that it was initially used as a national anthem by Luxembourg before being taken on by the USA!

Stroud Scarlet

What was STROUD SCARLET and why did it involve the talent of Gloucestershire's textile workers around the globe? Stroud Scarlet was once probably the most recognised colour in the world! The Stroud mills had a long-standing history of producing cloth of many different kinds and a great reputation for quality. They had perfected the art of producing scarlet cloth, with lengths of it being dried out in the local fields. This was known locally as Stroud Scarlet and it was used in army uniforms and in clothing worn by the royal family. The local workers also went on to make the cloth for the Royal Navy. The Stroud Valley was the hub for cloth-making in the 18th century because the area had an abundant supply of waterpower, powering no fewer than 150 mills. Today, Stroud still has a small textile industry, the results of which you may well have seen if you enjoy watching tennis or playing snooker! This is because it is home to factories which produce the baize (or Stroudwater baize) which covers snooker tables as well as the cloth that covers championship tennis balls. Both factories can trace their roots as far back as the Middle Ages. Another interesting fact about Stroud is that the British designer Jasper Conran once called it 'the Covent Garden of the Cotswolds'! It has also been dubbed one of the 'coolest towns in Britain' by the Sunday Times.

Michael Jackson and Gloucestershire

MICHAEL JACKSON and Gloucestershire may seem an unlikely combination, yet Gloucestershire was once featured in an unreleased song by the singer! The song, which was leaked onto the internet in March 2014, mainly became known for its unusual pronunciation of the county's name. *Days in*

Gloucestershire featured the artist pronouncing the county's name as 'Glue-kester-shire'. It is thought that Jackson recorded an initial version of the song in 2005, but never completed it before his untimely death in 2009.

The Domesday Book

WILLIAM THE CONQUEROR came to Gloucester in 1085 and while he was there he ordered that the **Domesday Book** should be written. This written record of a 'Great Survey' taken of England continues to be hugely important to this day. It was in Christmas in that year that William decided to send his men throughout England to discover the specific land and livestock held by each landholder. Written in Medieval Latin, the main aim of the Domesday Book was thought to be to uncover the taxes owed in King Edward the Confessor's reign. It now provides all kinds of invaluable insights into life in the past.

A tweet story

It is thanks to the humble pigeon that Cheltenham is said to owe its identity as a spa town. The story goes that local people kept noticing a big flock of pigeons gathering and pecking around a field close to the border of the town. When they looked a little more closely they discovered that the pigeons were congregating on the site of an old mineral spring. This is why you will find pigeons on the crest of Cheltenham.

The first lawnmower

Next time you mow the lawn, don't forget that it's a man from Gloucestershire that you have to thank for making your garden look better! This is because the very first lawnmower was invented in Stroud by an engineer called EDWIN BEARD BUDDING. The story goes that Budding was inspired to create his invention after seeing a machine in a local cloth mill using a cutting cylinder to create a smooth finish after the weaving process. He formed a partnership with another engineer and they went on to make lawnmowers in Stroud. You can see one of their earliest models, dating from 1830, at the Museum in the Park in Stroud.

iStock

The Harry Potter connection

If you're a fan of the *Harry Potter* books, you may already be aware of the link between the world of the bespectacled boy wizard and Gloucestershire. Not only was its creator J.K. ROWLING brought up in the Forest of Dean from the age of nine (and now lives in the county), but the atmospheric setting for the cloisters of Hogwarts School is none other than **Gloucester Cathedral**.

Gloucester Cathedral iStock

The country's longest river

Did you know that the principal river running through the county of Gloucestershire is the longest in Britain? The River

70

Severn is an impressive 220 miles (or 354 kilometres) long.

The Gloucestershire Old Spot

Gloucestershire Old Spot iStock

Gloucester isn't only famed for its sheep – its pigs are highly celebrated too! **The Gloucestershire Old Spot** has been the pig of the county for many years. It is easy to 'spot' because of its light pink colouring and large black patches – or spots! It's sometimes referred to as the *'Orchard Pig'* because it has a weakness for apples. The pig was actually officially named by the Gloucestershire Old Spots Breed Society, which was formed in 1913. They used the word 'old' in the animal's name as this type of pig has been around for as long as anyone can recall! According to the Gloucestershire Old Spots Breed Society, no other pedigree spotted breed was recorded before 1913, so today's spotted delight is the oldest of its kind in the world!

A Great history

Gloucestershire is understandably proud of its links with KING ALFRED THE GREAT. Born in Wantage in AD 849, the king changed British history for ever. As the King of Wessex from 871 to 899, Alfred defended his kingdom against the attack of the Vikings. He was so powerful a leader that he was the main ruler of England by the time he died. In fact, he's the only English monarch ever to be given the title '*the Great*'! This is not surprising when you consider that among his achievements Alfred successfully created a code of laws and an improved coinage system. He wasn't only talented at improving life for his subjects. He also developed himself through education, going on to learn Latin in his late thirties and becoming involved with translating books from Latin into Anglo-Saxon. Yet it is for his defence against the Vikings that he is best known. In fact, many historians say that if it wasn't for Alfred, there would be no England or English language! He is commemorated with a statue in Wantage town centre, marked with the inscription on the right:

Alfred found learning dead,
And he restored it.
Education neglected
And he revived it.
The laws powerless
And he gave them force.
The church debased
And he raised it.
The land ravaged by a fearful enemy,
From which he delivered it.
Alfred's name will live as long as mankind
shall respect the past.

Alfred the Great iStock

Alfred's importance was acknowledged by none other than Winston Churchill who, when he was told that he must be the greatest Englishman that ever lived, replied *'No! The greatest Englishman that ever lived was King Alfred.'*

King Alfred's daughter continued to make Gloucestershire proud. Æthelflæd, The Lady of the Mercians, ruled the Kingdom of Mercia from the Palace of Kingsholm and was buried at St Oswald's Priory. She is said to have been responsible for reconstructing Gloucester from a Roman ruin. She is also believed to have been the person who set out the core street plan for Gloucester which is still in use to this day.

An interesting postscript to this historic tale is that in January 2013, researchers discovered what they believe to be a fragment of pelvic bone belonging to either King Alfred or his son, Edward the Elder. The plan was to re-open a dig at Hyde Abbey Garden, where the bone was discovered. However, at the time of writing the dig is at a standstill because of issues between different groups involved with the project. If King Alfred the Great were alive today, perhaps he would have brought his wisdom to bear on the situation!

The dialect as spoken by the peasantry of Gloucestershire is not, as many suppose, mere vulgarisms. The tillers of the land many centuries ago, on the Cotteswold hills, spoke with the same impressiveness, power, and pathos as may still be heard in the retired rural districts of the county.

In the old words still in use, roots are discoverable from the Dutch, Saxon, Scandinavian, and Gaelic; but the great majority are Saxon.

As long ago as 1265 a work was written by Robert of Gloucester, in prose and verse, entitled 'Chronicles of Robert of Gloucester,' in the language still in use by the ploughboys of sequestered districts of the Cotteswolds.

This dialect is not peculiar to the county of Gloucester, but it is spoken in Wilts, Dorset, and parts of Somerset and Hants.

Excerpts from *A Glossary of Dialect and Archaic Words Used in the County of Gloucester* by J. DRUMMOND ROBERTSON, published 1890

Star Wars in Gloucestershire?

Star Wars is probably not the first thing that comes to mind when you think of Gloucestershire. Yet the county is now closely associated with the epic film series after scenes for the seventh Star Wars film were filmed in the Forest of Dean! The area of Puzzlewood in the Forest of Dean is no stranger to the film and TV world. It has also been a filming location for *Doctor Who*, *Merlin*, *Atlantis* and *Jack the Giant Slayer!*

The Doctor Who connection

Did you know that Gloucestershire has another link with the hugely popular series, *Doctor Who?* The fictional town of Leadworth, where the Doctor's companions and friends, AMY POND, RORY WILLIAMS and RIVER SONG come from, is meant to be located in Gloucestershire!

The Harkyhollurgists

Zum cwoaches druv to village church
In rare an' spankin style,
Wi' smokin' hosses vour in han',
From Cizeter dree mile.

Twur genelmen wi' boxers on
An' drest loik parsons all,
Wi' cwots zo black and chokers wite
An' zum wur short an' tall.

Tha gethered roun' the Churchyard Cross
An' pulled out aal thur books,
Tha ax'd his age, an' nun could tell:
Vive hundred yer he looks.

An' wen tha ax'd his age zo zolum
An' parsun shook ees hed;
Tha pwointed to the karven stwons
An' out a book tha red.

Ee thowt tha wur agwain to read
Th' sarvice over hee,
As parsun reds when volks be brot
And ded and cowld tha be.

At last a tall chap hollurs out
Let's march into the chirch,
Thur's more thur to tauk about
Vor which we are in zurch.

Excerpts from Legends, Tales, and Songs, in the Dialect of the Peasantry of Gloucestershire

Available now

Black Country Dialect

Bristol Dialect

Buckinghamshire Dialect

Cockney Dialect

Cornish Dialect

Derbyshire Dialect

Devon Dialect

Dorset Dialect

Essex Dialect

Evolving English WordBank

Glaswegian Dialect

Hampshire Dialect

Kent Dialect

Lancashire Dialect

Leicestershire Dialect

Liverpool Dialect

Manchester Dialect

Newcastle upon Tyne Dialect

Norfolk Dialect

Nottinghamshire Dialect

Scottish Dialects

Somerset Dialect

Sussex Dialect

The Lake District Dialect

Warwickshire Dialect

Wiltshire Dialect

Yorkshire Dialect

Coming in 2016

Co Durham Dialect

Wenglish Dialect

See website for more details: bradwellbooks.com

Sources

www.visitthecotswolds.org.uk

www.britishcheese.com/doublegloucester

www.bbc.co.uk/programmes

www.theguardian.com/commentisfree/2014/may/27/endangered-accents-english-language

www.deanweb.info/dennis%20potter.html

www.gloucestershireecho.co.uk/Michael-Jackson-song-Days-Gloucestershire-leaked/story-22282665-detail/story.html#ixzz3d8MoGVOK

www.essentialtravelguide.com/regional-guides/midlands/cotswolds-travel-guide/cotswolds-facts-figures/

www.dailymail.co.uk/news/article-2724024/Unknown-demo-song-Michael-Jackson-discovered-revealing-love-GLOUCESTERSHIRE-visited-child.html#ixzz3d8Me6XZh

www.gloucestercitizen.co.uk/County-rich-source-traditional-folk-music/story-17937093-detail/story.html#ixzz3bKziXill

www.bbc.co.uk/news/uk-england-gloucestershire-24865702

www.gloucestershiresociety.org.uk/The-Secrets-of-George-Ridler-s-Oven/the-secrets-of-george-ridler-s-oven.html

www.cityessence.co.uk/en/cities/gloucester

www.gospbc.co.uk/

www.bristolpost.co.uk/Reward-offer-secret-meanings-George-Ridler-s-Oven/story-19773955-detail/story.html

www.gloucestershiresociety.org.uk/History/George-Ridler-s-Oven/

www.bbc.co.uk/gloucestershire/content/articles/2009/05/05/
woolsack_races_history_feature.shtml

**www.gloucestercitizen.co.uk/Wacky-sayings-baffled/story-
11922575-detail/story.html**

www.oldlawnmowerclub.co.uk/aboutmowers/history#sthash.
SkHknEl1.dpuf

**www.gloucestershireecho.co.uk/Entire-population-tiny-
South-Pacific-island-speak/story-22211954-detail/story.html**

www.gloucestercitizen.co.uk/F-W-Harvey-Laureate-
Gloucestershire-WW1/story-21339282-detail/story.html

www.gloucestercitizen.co.uk/King-Alfred-Great-8217-s-links-
Gloucester/story-19619408-detail/story.html

**http://www.hampshirechronicle.co.uk/NEWS/11297104.
Duke_of_Gloucester_hears_latest_on_King_Alfred_the_
Great_project_at_Winchester_University/?ref=rss**

http://www.hampshirechronicle.co.uk/news/11660075.Dispute_
over_proposed_search_for_King_Alfred_bones/

**www.stroudnewsandjournal.co.uk/leisure/music/11406727.
Lottery_win_for_Gloucestershire_traditions/**

www.independent.co.uk/news/obituaries/winifred-foley-author-
whose-a-child-of-the-forest-put-the-forest-of-dean-on-the-literary-
map-1668045.html

**www.gloucestercitizen.co.uk/8203-Star-Wars-filming-boosts-
Gloucestershire/story-26596738-detail/story.html**

www.bbc.co.uk/news/uk-england-gloucestershire-29862707